DEATH ROW'S WILDEST WOMEN

Ty Treadwell

Copyright © 2016 Ty Treadwell

All rights reserved.

ISBN: 1533461414
ISBN-13: 978-1533461414

"I want to tell the world that I killed and robbed them, as cold as ice, and I'd do it again because I've hated human beings for a long time."
—Aileen Wuornos, executed in 2002 for killing six of her customers while working as a prostitute

"I hope they let me do my hair in jail. I would just die if my hair went to hell."
—Karla Homolka, a Canadian serial killer who partnered with her husband to rape and murder three girls

CONTENTS

Introduction	7
Michelle Michaud	11
Brittany Holberg	17
Eva Dugan	23
Brooke Rottiers	29
Sue Logue	34
Antoinette Frank	40
Suzanne Basso	46
Juanita Spinelli	52
Karla Faye Tucker	59
Martha Beck	66
Angelina Rodriguez	75
Christa Pike	82
Elizabeth Ann Duncan	89

Miss Runners-Up: The Women Who Didn't Quite Make It   96

Introduction

It's been nearly 100 years since the women's suffrage movement changed American society forever, but in many ways women are still fighting for equality. One notable case is on death row, where women make up less than 2% of the population despite committing roughly 11% of the murders. Only 51 women have been executed in the past century compared to over 1,400 men who have been executed since 1976 alone, and that trend shows no sign of changing anytime soon.

A mere 53 women are currently on death row in America, with a huge chunk of those—21 to be exact—incarcerated in California. Of the 30 other states where capital punishment is still practiced, half of them have no female death row inmates at all. The remaining states, with few exceptions, have only one or two condemned female prisoners each. To fully understand these meager numbers, let's look at them in sports terms. If America's prisons decided to form a softball league made up of female death row inmates, only California would have enough players for a full team. If a death row basketball league was organized instead, only four states (Alabama, California, Florida, and Texas) would have enough players to put on the court, but California would still be the only state to have reserve players coming off the bench. (Prison wardens, take note: due to the small pool of potential players, tennis and golf might be your best bet for all-female death row sports—as long as your "athletes" don't suddenly decide to use their racquets and golf clubs as makeshift weapons.) Men, on the other hand, are so common on death row that each state could easily put together multiple teams for Australian rules football (18 players per team) if desired—although even hardened criminals would probably complain about the level of violence in that brutal sport.

So why this disparity among the sexes? Are judges and juries simply more hesitant to mete out death sentences to women, or do females commit a different variety of murder which is kinder, gentler, and somehow less execution-worthy? Once upon a time, that might have been true. Although its popularity is waning these days, poison used to be quite popular among death row dames (and while death by poison is no walk in the park, it does lack the savagery that accompanies most stabbings, bludgeonings, and garden-variety shootings). Numerous women have also been convicted of orchestrating a murder rather than committing the killing themselves, leaving the victim dead while the female felon avoids getting her hands dirty (perhaps in the hopes of preserving an expensive manicure).

The most extreme difference between male and female killers, however, is in the choice of victims. Of the women currently on death row, half were convicted of killing their own husbands, their own children, or both. That means there's no reason to bolt your doors after reading this book, because the woman you really need to worry about is the one snuggled up beside you in bed or sitting across from you at the dinner table—which reminds me, you might want to check those mashed potatoes for arsenic and make sure there's no antifreeze in that glass of iced tea she just handed you with an adoring smile.

For the most part, that image of the poised, demure, and often grandmotherly female killer portrayed in Agatha Christie novels and countless TV dramas is a thing of the past, because today's homicidal women have gone that extra bloody mile to prove they're just as tough as the boys. These are the women who choose cutting-edge weapons over cutting-edge fashion, the women who scoff when someone says *You stab like a girl*. They demand equal sentences for equal crimes, they proudly break down traditional barriers (sometimes with a pickax or a sledgehammer), and they prefer to be labeled "pretty deadly" instead of just "pretty."

The women's rights movement has always embraced the slogan *Well-behaved women seldom make history.* In this book, you'll meet 13 women who would proudly wear those words across their blood-spattered t-shirts or slap a bumper sticker with that phrase on the car they just used to haul a dead body to the edge of town—right beside the sticker that says *A woman's place is in the death chamber* and below the one that states *I am woman, hear me roar (as I commit a gruesome murder)*.

Michelle Michaud

Today's busy woman-on-the-go needs to wear many hats and be adept at multi-tasking. Michelle Michaud proved she was capable of that by working as a school crossing guard, volunteering at a local church, and raising two kids as a single mom while still finding time to turn tricks at massage parlors and embark on a spree of serial kidnappings and rapes that resulted in the death of one of the victims.

Michaud began her adult life as a high school dropout who ran away from home and worked as a prostitute at a series of massage parlors and brothels in Nevada. She never married, but over the years Michaud gave birth to two children from two different men. Motherhood wasn't enough to lure Michaud away from the prostitution business, but she somehow managed to balance her two lives and even became an active member of her local church, organizing bake sales and luncheons by day and turning tricks for big money in the evening hours.

Michaud's carefully balanced life began to topple the day she met James Anthony Daveggio, nicknamed "Froggie" because of his deep, raspy voice. Froggie was a member of the Devil's Horsemen motorcycle club who had dyed his hair purple to match his motorcycle, a fashion statement that Michaud apparently found irresistible. The couple also shared a fondness for methamphetamine and violent sex, and love quickly blossomed between the rambunctious pair, which led to Froggie moving in with Michaud and her children. The home soon became known for its loud parties and frequent brawls, and the couple was evicted from their house after numerous complaints from the neighbors; that's when Froggie and Michaud transformed their wild, violent lifestyle from a neighborhood nuisance into a traveling road show.

Froggie had become obsessed with Gerald Gallego, dubbed the "Sex Slave Killer" by the press. With the help of his wife Charlene, Gallego had kidnapped, raped, and killed 10 young victims between 1978 and 1980. Froggie persuaded Michaud to help him emulate Gallego's crimes, and the two even dreamed of one day appearing on serial killer trading cards the way Gallego and his wife had. Using Michaud's

1994 Dodge Caravan as a mobile headquarters, the devious pair nabbed their first victim—a 20-year-old college student—in September 1997. Froggie forced the girl into the van then raped her repeatedly while Michaud drove. Unlike Gerald Gallego, however, Froggie released his victim after the assault.

Over the next two months, the evil couple embarked on a kidnap-and-rape spree that would claim at least half a dozen more victims. "Much as some people might go duck hunting, these people went hunting for women who were vulnerable to abduction," said Pleasanton Police Chief Bill Eastman. "They knew what they were doing. It was quite premeditated and vicious in the way they carried it out." Froggie modified Michaud's van by removing the rear seats and installing a system of hooks and ropes, turning the vehicle into what Eastman would later describe as a "murder and abduction chamber." Some of the victims were strangers while others weren't; at one point, Michaud even lured one of her teenage daughter's friends to the van with the promise of drugs, then helped Froggie assault her.

On Thanksgiving Day, Froggie and Michaud won a gold medal for Most Awkward Conversation at the Holiday Dining Table by trying to enlist Froggie's daughter as a sidekick to help them choose, kidnap, and possibly even kill their next victim. According to the girl, Michaud claimed that since the day after Thanksgiving was the biggest shopping day of the year, it would also be the best day to commit rape and murder—lending new meaning to the term Black Friday.

Froggie's daughter turned down the bizarre offer, and it would end up being five more days until Froggie and Michaud claimed the most decisive victim in their months-long crime spree. On December 2, the pair kidnapped 22-year-old Vanessa Lei Samson as the girl walked to work early in the morning. Froggie was now determined to escalate his crimes to the level of Gerald Gallego's, and over the course of 35 hours Samson was raped, tortured, then strangled with a nylon cord before her body was dumped onto a snowy embankment beside the road.

Ironically, the killers were arrested the next day on charges of assault and kidnapping based on evidence given to police by Froggie and Michaud's first rape victim. A search of the modified Dodge Caravan revealed ropes, a ball gag, a porn tape titled *Submissive Young Girls*, true crime books, serial killer trading cards, and two curling irons that had been used during the sexual torture of Vanessa Lei Samson. Since Samson's body hadn't been discovered, however, the items didn't yet carry their damning weight.

While she lingered in jail after the arrest for assault and kidnapping, Michaud saw a news broadcast about the discovery of Samson's body. She confided to a new prison pal that she had been involved in the crime, and the jailhouse snitch immediately passed the information on to prison authorities. Froggie and Michaud were both charged with murder, and although each claimed the other had actually killed the girl, both were found guilty and both received the death penalty. At the sentencing, Alameda County Superior Court Judge Larry Goodman stated that execution was the only fitting punishment for a crime that was "vile, cruel, senseless, depraved, brutal, evil, and vicious." (Ironically, these were also the names of the seven dwarves in an earlier version of *Snow White* that Disney decided not to release after test audiences ran screaming from the theater.)

Froggie and Michaud have been languishing on California's death row since 2002; the state has currently put its executions on hold due to litigation involving the lethal injection procedure, so the Golden State's death row inmates might be more likely to die of old age rather than by their court-ordered decrees. In the meantime, Michelle Michaud has switched from trolling for victims to trolling for pen pals. Her contact information appears on several websites designed to connect death row inmates with those outside the prison walls, and Michaud begins one of her ads by lamenting *Sometimes it feels the whole world has forgotten me. It would be nice to hear my name at mail call.*

Brittany Holberg

Some women go through outfit after outfit while preparing for a date, trying on every stitch of clothing in their closet before they find the perfect fit. Brittany Holberg did the same thing with weapons when she committed murder, using practically every household item but the kitchen sink until her poor victim finally succumbed to his injuries.

Before she landed on death row, Holberg's life was already a series of trials and tribulations. Her father was a heroin addict who was in and out of prison, so Holberg was raised by her mother—who worked as a sheriff's deputy—and her stepfather. When Holberg was 12 years old, one of her aunts was murdered. The family spiraled into depression, and Holberg claims her parents began to drink heavily, smoke marijuana, and abuse prescription drugs. "They would pass out on the couch," she said. "They wouldn't know where they were. They were so drunk." Holberg claims her parents even offered marijuana to her at the tender age of 10.

Holberg ran away from her home in Amarillo, Texas, when she was 16. She and the boy she would later marry traveled to California where Holberg gave birth to a daughter, but the marriage didn't last long and Holberg eventually moved back home. She had developed bad habits of her own by then, and was addicted to prescription drugs she started taking following a knee injury. A relative taught her how to scam dentists into writing her prescriptions for opiate-based drugs, and soon Holberg was taking as many as 100 pills a day along with cocaine. When methadone treatment failed to cure her drug problems, Holberg sent her daughter to live with her grandmother and began working full time to feed her addiction. She danced at strip clubs, wrote bad checks, committed forgery, used stolen credit cards, and eventually turned to prostitution.

Holberg was pursuing her trade in the world's oldest profession when she met her victim, although the accounts of that meeting vary widely from person to person. The official story is that Holberg had been in a car accident, saw an elderly man named A.B. Towery Sr. walking home after a trip to the grocery store, and asked the man if she could come inside and use his phone. Once inside the apartment, Holberg began smoking crack. Towery got mad, hit Holberg twice on the head with a metal pan, and a fight ensued. Holberg, on the other hand, claimed that Towery was a frequent customer who paid her for sex on a regular basis, and that when she asked him for extra money, he flew into a rage and attacked her.

Regardless of how it began, the argument between Holberg and Towery turned into a knock-down, drag-out brawl that lasted 45 minutes and ended with Towery dead on the floor. During the fight, Holberg stabbed her victim with a butcher knife, a grapefruit knife, and two forks. She also strangled him with a cord and beat him with a hammer, a skillet, a steam iron, and a space heater. Finally, as a coup de grace, Holberg shoved a foot-long lamp pole nearly halfway down Towery's throat. Once Towery was dead, Holberg took a shower, changed into clean clothes, stole Towery's money and some of his prescription drugs, then fled the scene. She used the stolen cash to fund a weekend-long cocaine binge, but had to cut the party short when she discovered that she had been linked to the murder by fingerprints and palm prints left at the scene. Holberg hitched a ride to Tennessee as a last-ditch escape attempt, but was soon arrested by Memphis police after an informant saw her and recognized her picture from the TV news.

The resulting trial was bizarre and chaotic. Holberg's attorneys claimed that Towery started the fight and that Holberg was merely defending herself—by stabbing her 80-year-old victim 58 times then beating him with every object she could get her hands on. They also claimed that Towery had a violent past and was prone to fits of sudden anger. The prosecution, on the other hand, painted Holberg as a carnage-loving woman who had decimated her victim with maniacal glee. "I suspect that the lamp stand was unnecessary," remarked a court psychiatrist as he described the intensity of Holberg's attack and the wide range of weapons she used. When asked if Holberg might have stuffed the lamp down her victim's throat by accident, a medical examiner shook his head and replied, "I think it was forced down there." (This begs the question of whether lamp-related choking accidents are common in that part of Texas. *Honest, sheriff, I was just using that lamp to swat a fly off his face when the dad-gum thing went halfway down his throat!*)

The defense fought an uphill battle; the fellow prostitutes they called to testify were supposed to back up Holberg's story about Towery being a regular customer with violent tendencies, but these witnesses came across as "drug addicted or marginally credible," as one newspaper noted, while the prosecution's witnesses appeared to be slightly less wasted and slightly more believable. The most damning evidence came from Vicki Kirkpatrick, who had befriended Holberg at a felony drug treatment center; according to Kirkpatrick, Holberg bragged that she enjoyed killing Towery and that his blood was pretty, like a fountain, as it left his body. "She stuffed that lamp thing down his throat because she got tired of hearing him making the noises," Kirkpatrick added.

Swayed by the jailhouse confession and the violent nature of the crime, Holberg was found guilty of murder and sentenced to die. She has lived on death row since 1998, occasionally popping up to file an appeal or complain about her treatment.

While the jury didn't care for Holberg, she obviously has her fans. The convicted killer appeared on an internet list of death row's most attractive inmates, and was also included in the feature story "Babes Behaving Badly" in the popular men's magazine Maxim. Other publications devoted to the female form would probably love to run pictorials of

Holberg, but her current prison surroundings only allow one form of photography: cell-fies.

Eva Dugan

Johnny Appleseed. Annie Oakley. Davey Crockett. America loves its folk heroes, those men and women whose real-life exploits ballooned into the stuff of myth and legend over time to create characters larger than life. Eva Dugan can be added to that list as well, because even though Dugan was a convicted killer unknown for any heroics—real or imagined—her story is a spicy stew of fact, conjecture, and urban folklore, all blended together to form one of the most memorable women in the annuls of American crime and punishment.

Dugan's early years are shrouded in mystery; she was born sometime between 1876 and 1878 and supposedly married when she was sixteen years old, giving birth to two children soon after. Some say Dugan grew up in Alaska while others say she traveled there during the time of the Klondike Gold Rush to work as a cabaret singer and prostitute who went by the nickname "Claw-Finger Kitty." Little is known of Dugan's adventures in the decades afterward, with most of the surviving information taking place between 1926 and 1930.

Dugan eventually left Alaska and made her way to Tucson, Arizona, where she began working as a housekeeper for a wealthy chicken rancher named Andrew Mathis in early 1927. But the two quarreled constantly, and after a short time—some say two weeks, others say two months—Dugan was fired. Within days, Mathis went missing along with his car and some of his possessions. Dugan claimed the rancher had moved to California, but his friends found it odd that the elderly man would just pack up and leave without telling anyone. When the local sheriff began investigating the disappearance, he found that Mathis's cashbox was missing. He also learned that Eva Dugan had recently sold off some of Mathis's belongings to other Tucson residents. The sheriff and his men searched Mathis's property, but found nothing odd except a charred ear trumpet thought to belong to the missing rancher, who was hard of hearing.

Since Dugan had also disappeared by then, the sheriff began digging into her background and discovered that Eva had been married five times during her life, and that all five husbands had vanished without a trace just like Mathis had. Following a trail of postcards Dugan had sent to friends, the sheriff finally tracked the missing woman down in New York and was able to extradite her back to Tucson when he found out Dugan was in possession of Mathis's car. But with the rancher still missing and no signs of foul play, the worst crime Dugan could be charged with was grand larceny. That situation changed, however, when a traveler passing through the area came across a skeleton in the desert outside Tucson—and that skeleton happened to be wearing a set of dentures custom-made for Andrew Mathis, as was verified by the local dentist who fashioned them.

Dugan was tried for murder, but she quickly passed the blame by claiming a mysterious cowhand known only as "Jack" had committed the crime. Dugan said that Jack was her lover, and that the cowhand got into a fight with Mathis and killed the old man by punching him in the heart. Afterward, Jack supposedly helped Dugan bury Mathis in the desert before he fled across the border to Mexico. The jury was more than dubious; no one else in town had ever seen or heard of a cowhand named Jack, and no proof of his existence could be located. After a short two-day trial, the jury found Dugan guilty of murder and the judge sentenced her to hang—the first such sentence ever handed down to a woman in the state of Arizona.

Dugan kept a stiff upper lip after her sentence was read, telling the jurors, "Well, I'll die with my boots on and in full health. And that's more than most of you old coots will be able to boast on."

Several appeals were filed on Dugan's behalf over the following years, but these proved fruitless. Dugan also lost a bid to have her guilty verdict thrown out by reason of insanity, despite the support of the prison warden, who believed Dugan's "moral attitude, violent temper, and ravenous appetite" were proof of her mental instability. "Her thinking is immoral," he commented. "Her thoughts were only of men, money, and food."

While awaiting her execution day, Dugan gave interviews for one dollar apiece and sold handkerchiefs she embroidered in her cell to save up money for her burial costs. She also spent the time sewing beads and artificial flowers onto her burial shroud, turning the bleak garment into a fancy jazz-style dress. On the eve before her execution, Dugan was allowed to host a card game with three female friends. And even though she had previously dismissed the idea of a last meal, calling it "phony," she changed her mind at the last minute and requested a can of oysters, a can of milk, and some crackers, which she used to cook an oyster stew on a small stove inside her cell.

While Dugan seemed resigned to her fate, rumors swirled that she might take her own life rather than allow herself to be executed. Hours before her hanging, guards searched her cell and found razor blades and a small bottle of either poison or raw ammonia. But Dugan appeared stoic and carefree as she was led to the gallows later that morning, kissing two of her guards goodbye and saying, "I love everyone connected with the prison. You have all been good to me, and I can't blame you for what the law is going to do to me."

After giving the jailhouse preacher her dentures for safekeeping, Dugan calmly climbed the steps to the gallows platform. Guards placed straps around her shoulders, hips, knees, and ankles, then pulled a black hood over her head before they slipped the noose around her neck and tightened it. Moments later a switch was thrown, the trap door beneath Dugan's feet opened, and the condemned woman plunged downward. Unfortunately, however, the executioner had miscalculated the rope length and Dugan's head snapped clean off and rolled toward a group of execution witnesses, which prompted a fair amount of fainting. Because of the messy debacle, Dugan became the first and last woman to be hanged in Arizona, which adopted the gas chamber as its method of execution just three years later.

Brooke Rottiers

Newspapers love coming up with nicknames for female murderers, and the melodrama nearly drips off the page when they write about women such as the Duchess of Death, the Killer Granny, The Tigress, or the Black Widow. But Brooke Rottiers came up with her own nickname, something short and simple that perfectly describes her behavior during the double murder she committed: Crazy. And this wasn't one of those cases where someone makes a breezy statement like *Call me crazy, but I'm really starting to enjoy Justin Bieber's music.* Rottiers used her questionable nickname often—and proudly—and it even appeared on one of her utility bills instead of her real name.

In 2006, Rottiers was a single mother of four working part-time as a prostitute and living in a fleabag motel in Corona, California, with Omar Tyree Hutchinson, a small-time drug dealer. Rumor had it, however, that Rottiers preferred to rob her customers rather than have sex with them, and because she was six feet tall and weighed 200 pounds, it's easy to imagine Rottiers strong-arming a nervous john.

One hot August day, Rottiers was drinking in a bar with a female friend, Franchune Dyuel Epps, when the two women met up with a pair of day laborers. Rottiers chatted the men up and revealed her occupation, then enticed them back to her motel with the promise of sex for money. But Rottiers's brutal treatment of the men turned the world's oldest profession into the world's coldest profession, and police later cobbled together a description of the events based on testimony from Hutchinson, Epps, and other guests who were staying at the motel at the time.

Once they reached the motel, the two day laborers quickly learned that an evening of romance was out of the question. Hutchinson and two of Rottiers's young daughters were waiting in the room, where the men were forced to undress. Rottiers began hitting them with her fists and a belt, knocking one of them out, and Hutchinson allegedly took a few swings as well. Rottiers then gagged both men and tied them up using anything she could get her hands on; phone cords, belts, underwear, one of her bras, pink duct tape, and the power cord for a vacuum cleaner, among other items. Once the men were lying beaten and helpless on the floor, Epps claims that Rottiers smothered them by standing on their faces with her bare feet for as long as ten to fifteen minutes, until their skin turned purple.

The woman had no soul, but she obviously had formidable soles.

The men eventually succumbed to their injuries, although the exact method of death is unclear. Both died from asphyxiation, but since both had so many different items tied around their necks and one had a plastic bag over his head, it's difficult to tell if Rottiers ended the men's lives with her hands, her feet, or one of the foreign objects. Afterward, Rottiers and Epps wrapped the bodies in motel sheets, loaded them into a car, and drove to a remote area near a lake. They tried to light the car on fire but failed, and wound up abandoning it instead.

Police discovered the car and the bodies the next day. Both men were still tied up with an assortment of phone cords, electrical cords, bras, and underwear, and one of the men had a pair of panties shoved down his throat. The logical deduction at that point would have been to search for a bipolar killer who worked part-time at Radio Shack and part-time at Victoria's Secret. Instead, police figured out that the sheets the bodies were wrapped in had come from a hotel and began a search of local establishments. That search eventually led to the National Inn, a seedy joint frequented by parolees, prostitutes, and drug dealers. Investigators learned that Rottiers and Hutchinson had recently been evicted from their room when hotel maids discovered that bedsheets were missing and that the power cords from two vacuum cleaners owned by the hotel had been removed. They also interviewed other guests at the motel who revealed that Rottiers had shared details about the murders, including the fact the she enjoyed strangling the men with her bras and panties and that she switched to hitting them with her fists when they "started to smell."

Rottiers, Hutchinson, and Epps were all arrested and each was tried by a separate jury. Hutchinson and Epps admitted to helping dispose of the bodies, but denied involvement in the robbery and murder of the two victims. All three were found guilty, and Hutchinson and Epps were sentenced to life in prison without parole. Rottiers, on the other hand, was given the death penalty for being the mastermind and primary offender in a double murder that the judge called "cold, callous, brutal, and particularly cruel."

Call me crazy, but I tend to agree with him.

Sue Logue

Some condemned criminals dream of their lavish last meal. Others eagerly look forward to visiting with family members before their execution. And all would probably relish the chance for one last roll in the hay before they embark on their permanent date with the Grim Reaper, but that luxury is normally out of the question—which makes the story of Sue Logue that much more unique.

The long and sordid chain of events that led Logue to the electric chair began in a broad, windswept South Carolina field in 1940. A mule belonging to rural store owner Davis Timmerman somehow wandered onto the property of farmer Wallace Logue, Sue's husband. The mule kicked a calf belonging to Logue, killing it, and Logue demanded that the other man pay him $20 in restitution money. Timmerman agreed, but when Wallace Logue visited Timmerman's general store to collect his payment, he upped his demand to $40 instead. Timmerman refused to pay such an exorbitant amount, which infuriated Wallace Logue. (Historians wonder if Timmerman might have tried to calm Logue down by telling him, *Don't have a cow, man*, to which Logue might have replied, *I don't have a cow, you idiot, and it's all the fault of your accursed mule!*)

In a fit of rage, Wallace Logue grabbed a nearby ax handle and started thrashing Timmerman with it. Timmerman then scrambled for a pistol he kept in a drawer for protection and shot Logue to death. Afterward, the injured store owner drove to the local sheriff's office to report the incident. A trial was held, but Timmerman was released after the jury ruled that he acted in self-defense.

The widow Sue Logue was furious that the man who killed her husband had been set free and decided to take the law into her own hands. She and George Logue, Wallace's brother, paid Wallace's nephew Joe Frank Logue to find someone to kill Timmerman. Despite the fact that Joe Frank was a police officer, he agreed to the plan and enlisted an out-of-work plasterer named Clarence Bagwell to perform the hit. Joe Frank drove Bagwell to Timmerman's store, then waited in the car while Bagwell went inside and shot Timmerman five times from close range, killing him.

The pair might have gotten away with the crime, too, if not for an ironic turn of events; Bagwell, who normally did the plastering, got plastered himself at a bar one night and drunkenly bragged to a lady friend about earning big money for killing a man. That lady friend took her story to the police, who pulled Bagwell in for questioning. The nervous killer confessed to the crime and blew the whistle on Joe Frank Logue as well. Equally nervous and equally loose-lipped, Joe Frank told the cops that Sue Logue and George Logue were the masterminds behind the plan.

What happened next resembled a Wild West shootout from the frontier days. Sheriff Wad Allen and Deputy Doc Clark headed to Sue Logue's home to arrest her and George, but the pair somehow learned the lawmakers were coming and set up an ambush. George Logue and his friend Fred Dorn exchanged gunfire with the sheriff and deputy, and when the smoke finally cleared, the sheriff lay dead and the three other men had all been wounded. Deputy Clark managed to get away and report the incident, and in no time at all Sue Logue's house was surrounded by dozens of lawmen with firearms drawn.

This is where a weird story gets even weirder.

Instead of turning the Logue home into Swiss cheese with a hail of bullets, officials asked a local circuit court judge who was a friend of the Logue family to appeal for a surrender. That judge happened to be Strom Thurmond, future governor of South Carolina and future state senator. Rumor had it that Thurmond and Sue Logue had been having an affair when she was a teacher and he was a school superintendent. Rumor also had it that Sue Logue was a hellcat in the bedroom, and that Thurmond—along with other men—had been blissfully devastated by her sexual prowess. But in this incident, it was Thurmond who turned on the charm and convinced Sue Logue, George Logue, and Fred Dorn to surrender.

Within two days, Fred Dorn and Deputy Clark both succumbed to the injuries they sustained during the shootout. That meant two lawmen had died while trying to arrest Sue and George for the murder of Davis Timmerman. Prosecutors honed in on Sue Logue at the ensuing trial, but instead of ranting about her evil brain or her cold heart, they blamed her lawless behavior on another organ by proclaiming, "Oh, what a line of murder and assassination have come from the spleen of that mastermind." (Although stricken from newspaper accounts, the lawyer supposedly went on to describe Logue's "wicked kidneys" and "devilish pancreas" before proclaiming that the woman's list of vile indiscretions would stretch farther than her small intestine.)

The trial lasted only three days, with the jury deliberating for a measly two hours before finding Sue Logue, George Logue, and Clarence Bagwell guilty of murder. The trio were sentenced to death, with the executions taking place a scant ten months after their guilty verdicts were read. (Sue's nephew Joe Frank was found guilty and received a death sentence as well, but his was commuted to life in prison only hours before his execution).

Not much is known about the short time Sue Logue spent in the women's penitentiary prior to her execution, but the execution day itself has become legendary. Remarkably, Strom Thurmond was allowed to ride with Logue in the back of the car as she was driven from the women's penitentiary to the main prison where executions took place. The driver of the car would later report that Thurmond and Logue were "hugging and kissing" the whole time, although other law enforcement officials surmise that the pair went further than standard first date shenanigans and that the driver had merely chosen his words carefully. In other words, the phrase *Wow, Sue Logue really banged Judge Thurmond's gavel* did not mean that the condemned woman was allowed to handle the items the future senator used in the courtroom.

Sue Logue probably went to the electric chair with a smile on her face—although the same can't be said of George Logue and Clarence Bagwell, who were executed in the same chair less than an hour later. The only tingling those two felt in their groins would have come from the lethal dose of electricity each received.

Antoinette Frank

It's always bad when a police officer commits a crime, and it's even worse when a police officer commits a crime together with a known felon. But when a police officer commits a crime together with a known felon and then shows up at the crime scene a few hours later to investigate that crime in front of witnesses who observed that crime, and the police officer acts as if nothing happened, things go from bad to worse to just plain wacky. Such was the case with Antoinette Frank, who probably committed more crimes than she solved during her short stint in uniform.

Frank was born and raised in Opelousas, Louisiana, and dreamed of being a police officer before she was even old enough to drive. At age 16, she joined a program designed to teach young people about police department operations. By the time she turned 21, Frank was ready to apply to the New Orleans

Police Department despite the potential stumbling blocks that might prevent her from being hired. The first of these popped up during a background investigation, when the police discovered that Frank's brother was wanted on attempted manslaughter charges and that Frank herself had been fired from a local Wal-Mart because of "personality conflicts," something Frank lied about on her police application. The results of her assessment and personality tests were bleak as well; Frank was ranked as "poor" in the areas of tolerance, impulse control, and open-mindedness, and as "below average" in stability and maturity. The psychiatrist who evaluated Frank found her lacking in many of the core abilities needed to be a police officer, and determined that she was unsuitable for the job.

Frank was crushed by the results of her evaluation, but it turned out there was no cause for worry. The NOPD was so shorthanded—and so desperate to bring more African-American females onto the force—that Frank was hired despite having zero qualifications. She graduated from the Police Academy in 1993, then began her very short and completely disastrous career as an officer of the New Orleans Police Department.

In late 1994, Frank was sent to investigate a shooting incident. One of the wounded victims at the scene was Rogers LaCaze, a known drug dealer with a violent past. Frank was instantly smitten with the barely-18-year-old thug; maybe it was his boyish good looks, or his shiny gold teeth, or the combination of his baggy pants and gangsta charm. Frank helped LaCaze get the medical care he needed, and the two became inseparable afterward. Frank let LaCaze tag along with her on the job, sometimes introducing him to others as a trainee, other times saying he was her nephew. She also let LaCaze drive her patrol car and used her status as a cop to help LaCaze out whenever he got in a fight or needed protection during his "business deals." The pair were even suspected of committing a string of small-time robberies and shakedowns together, with Frank pinning the crimes on others.

But those petty offenses were nothing compared to the crime that landed both Frank and LaCaze on death row. Just before 2 a.m. on March 4, 1995, Frank and LaCaze visited Kim Anh, a family-run Vietnamese restaurant. Frank had been moonlighting there as a late night security guard for months, but that night one of her fellow NOPD officers, Ronald Williams, was working the security detail instead.

When Frank used a key to let herself in, 23-year-old Chau Vu instinctively knew something was wrong. Frank had already come to the restaurant twice that evening to chow down on some leftover food, and there was no reason for the woman to return at such a late hour. The Vu family had also never given Frank a key, making her casual entrance even more strange.

Chau went to the kitchen, where her sister Ha and her brother Cuong were cleaning up, and put away the money she had been counting. Because the Vu family didn't trust banks, there was over $10,000 in cash on hand at the time. Chau shoved the bills into the microwave then returned to the dining room, where Frank and LaCaze had been confronted by Ronald Williams and Chau's other brother Quoc. As Frank shoved Chau and Quoc into the kitchen, LaCaze pulled out a gun and shot Williams three times, killing him. Chau and Quoc ran through the kitchen to a walk-in cooler at the back and hid inside, peeking through the glass door to see what was happening. Chau had yelled for her other brother and her sister to follow her into the cooler, but Ha and Cuong were frozen in place. Frank and LaCaze searched the kitchen until they found the money, then Frank executed Ha and Cuong with a total of 10 gunshots as the brother and sister knelt on the floor. After a quick, fruitless search for Chau and Quoc, the pair of killers got in their car and sped away.

Chau and Quoc called 911 and remained hidden in the cooler while they waited for the police to arrive—and to their amazement, Antoinette Frank was the first officer on the scene. She had dropped LaCaze off at his apartment, swung by the police station to swap her car for a patrol car, then sped back to the restaurant to see if she could find the two remaining witnesses. But a second car with two more officers inside pulled up minutes later, before Frank could eliminate the brother and sister. Chau rushed out of the cooler and ran to the other officers, sobbing and pleading for help. In an insane attempt to act calm and nonchalant, Frank asked Chau to explain what happened. "You know what happened!" Chau blurted to the crooked cop. "You were there!"

Frank was immediately detained and later arrested, and LaCaze—who brought attention to himself by buying gas with a credit card he stole from Ronald Williams's wallet after he shot him—was taken into custody a short time later. At first, Frank and LaCaze blamed each other for the shootings. Then Frank admitted that she had killed Ha and Cuong, but claimed that LaCaze masterminded the robbery and forced her to shoot the brother and sister. With two eyewitness accounts and a mountain of other evidence against them, however, Frank and LaCaze didn't have a leg to stand on.

Both killers were charged with three counts of first-degree murder and given separate trials. LaCaze went first, and his jury found him guilty and sentenced him to death. At Frank's trial, her lawyers didn't call a single witness or present a single piece of evidence; their sole argument was that the prosecution hadn't proven its case beyond a reasonable doubt. The jury dismissed this Hail Mary legal tactic, and in record time to boot. They needed just 22 minutes to find Frank guilty on all charges and an extra 45 minutes to sentence her to death.

Both Frank and LaCaze remain on death row to this day, although LaCaze has recently lobbied for a new trial and might actually get one. Frank seems to have no such option, however, and has gone from wearing blue to feeling blue as the endless days tick by on Louisiana's death row.

Suzanne Basso

Scientists have debated the existence of a "murder gene" for years, but in Suzanne Basso's case, the evidence is fairly compelling. Basso's uncle was Robert Garrow, a farmer's son who spent his early years practicing bestiality with farm animals and gratifying himself with milking machines before he grew up to become a rapist and spree killer who took the lives of four victims. And while Basso didn't share her uncle's affection for livestock, she did engage in behavior that was quite animalistic.

Basso was born in New York in 1954, married as a teenager, and gave birth to two children before she turned 20. She and her family relocated to Houston, Texas, where Basso would meet the man whose name she would eventually take. Although she was still married, Suzanne allowed a man named Carmine Basso to move into the family home. And although she couldn't legally marry a second time,

Suzanne did post a wedding announcement in the local paper stating that Suzanne Margaret Anne Cassandra Lynn Theresa Marie Mary Veronica Sue Burns-Standlinslowski, a former nun, former gymnast, and heiress to a Nova Scotia oil fortune, would soon be wed to Carmine Joseph John Basso (the newspaper retracted the ad three days later on the basis that it might contain inaccuracies). Carmine Basso would mysteriously die from erosion of the esophagus less than two years later, although police ruled the death to be from natural causes.

Since one husband had died and the other had left home, Basso found herself alone. But the "grieving widow" soon met another man, a grocery store bagboy named Louis "Buddy" Musso. Basso was on vacation in New Jersey, and she ran into Musso at a church bazaar. Musso was mentally challenged, with the intellect of a young child, but he had been married previously and lost his wife to cancer. Since then, the lonely Musso had been looking for the next love of his life. Basso seemed to fit that bill perfectly, and after she returned to Houston, Musso began making plans to follow her. Since Musso had always longed to become a country western singer, a move to Texas would be a dream come true. Unfortunately for Musso, that dream quickly turned into a nightmare.

Dressed like an old-time cowboy in his ten-gallon hat, neckerchief, and boots, Musso traveled to Texas to move in with his wife-to-be. But soon after he arrived, Basso tried to gain access to Musso's social security payments and also took out an insurance policy on her "future husband" that would pay her $65,000 in the event that Musso died as the result of a violent crime. It didn't take long before Basso herself orchestrated and took part in that very crime.

From the time Musso moved in with Basso, he was abused and treated like a slave by Basso and her friends. He was given endless household chores to perform, and would be beaten or kicked if he didn't complete them fast enough. Sometimes Basso, who weighed 300 pounds at that point, would even jump up and down on her hapless suiter. Basso also denied Musso food and water, didn't let him use the bathroom, and would force him to kneel on a floor mat for hours. If Musso tried to leave the floor mat, he would be beaten by Basso or a member of her gang of thugs, which included Basso's son James, a woman named Bernice Ahrens, Bernice's son Craig and daughter Hope, and Hope's boyfriend Terence Singleton. Neighbors noticed Musso's black eyes and other injuries, but no one bothered to call the police.

On one occasion when Musso was out in public and a police officer noticed the man's scrapes and bruises, Musso claimed that he had been beaten up by Mexicans.

Less than three months after he moved to Texas, Musso's life ended in a night of violence. The tragic event supposedly began when Musso broke a Mickey Mouse ornament at the apartment where Bernice Ahrens lived with her children and her daughter's boyfriend. Hope Ahrens started beating Musso with a wooden bird, and soon the others joined in. Musso was beaten with various objects including a belt, a baseball bat, and a vacuum cleaner, and he was also punched and kicked repeatedly. Afterward, Musso lay dying on the floor. When he begged someone to call an ambulance, his request was denied. After Basso left for work, her son doused Musso with bleach and other household cleaners then scrubbed his body with a wire brush. By the time Basso came home again, Musso was dead.

Police found Musso's body dumped by the side of the road a few days later. He was covered with hundreds of bruises in addition to lash marks from a whip and burns that might have come from a cigarette or a hot poker. Musso also had over 40 cuts on his head and body, 14 broken ribs, a fractured skull, a broken nose, two dislocated vertebrae, and a fractured bone in his neck.

Basso had filed a missing person report on Musso, claiming he had run away from home with a "little Mexican lady," but when police asked Basso and her son James to identify the body, James immediately confessed to the murder. The Ahrens family coughed up additional details of the sordid crime, and soon the entire gang was arrested.

Everyone pegged Basso as the mastermind behind the torture and killing. Perhaps in the hope of gaining pity, the cruel woman invented countless stories about the awful treatment she received in prison while awaiting her trial. At one point, she claimed to be paralyzed from the chest down due to a jailhouse beating. She also complained about losing her vision, and once accused a prison nurse of trying to kill her by smuggling a venomous snake into the jail inside a hollowed-out copy of a Roy Rogers biography. As a last-ditch effort, Basso began speaking in a squeaky child's voice during court appearances in an attempt to make it look like she had mentally regressed. Basso doubled down on that pretense of mental instability by also claiming to be a triplet, a former employee of New York's governor, and a past girlfriend of Nelson Rockefeller.

None of her ruses were successful, however, and Basso was found guilty of murder and sentenced to death while her son and the other members of her gang of thugs were given prison terms ranging from 80 years to life. Basso was executed on February 5, 2014.

Buddy Musso's tragic death is such a melancholy tale that it could easily be immortalized in one of the classic country western songs Musso loved so dearly. After a slight adjustment of the facts and with an added dose of Texas twang, I can picture a cowboy from one of those old black and white movies singing a tune that goes something like this:

Basso killed Musso and she made quite a mess-o,

She choked him with a lasso then drank an espresso,

Yippie-yi, yippie-yi-yo-ki-yay.

Juanita Spinelli

A mouse wearing glasses sounds awfully cute, like something from a Disney cartoon or a picture you'd see on a sign in the children's section of the library. But Juanita Spinelli, who was once compared to a mouse wearing glasses because of her big ears, long nose, and curly brown hair, was anything but cute. The female crime boss—whose snooty personality earned her the nickname the Duchess—was actually one tough customer. The same prison warden who made the mouse comparison went on to say this about Spinelli after her death: "She was the coldest, hardest character, male or female, that I had ever known, and was utterly lacking in feminine appeal. The Duchess was a hag, as evil as a witch. Horrible to look at, impossible to like, but she was still a woman, and I dreaded the thought of ordering her execution." But order it he did, making Spinelli the first woman to die in California's gas chamber and, at that time, the first woman executed by the state in any fashion in nearly 100 years.

Spinelli was born in Kentucky in 1889, but she developed wanderlust at a young age and dabbled in plenty of other occupations before she finally settled down as a career criminal. She apparently married and divorced several times during these early years, dragging her children along with her as she meandered from state to state. She washed clothes and waited tables in Texas, worked as a sheepherder in Idaho, and operated a gambling wheel at a Utah carnival where she also secured her teenage daughter Lorraine, who went by the nickname of "Gypsy," a gig as a snake charmer. Rumor had it that Spinelli also worked as a wrestler, a professional knife thrower, and the madam of a brothel at various points in her life, but the woman didn't truly find her calling until she dove head-first into the seedy underworld of organized crime.

Allegedly involved with notorious gangster organizations such as the Purple Gang and the Red Cap Gang, Spinelli founded her own band of criminals in San Francisco in the late 1930s. The group included Spinelli's common-law husband Michael Simeone, a young car thief named Gordon Hawkins, a teenage delinquent named Robert

Sherrod, and a one-eyed, slightly insane hood named Albert Ives. Spinelli's daughter Gypsy was also part of the gang, while her younger children tagged along on some of the gang's adventures without actually taking part. "I don't believe in keeping anything from children," Spinelli said, treating her two young sons like small adults, although she did set limits when it came to things like serving alcohol to the wee ones. "I don't believe in too many cocktails for little chaps," the Duchess explained. "One or two mild whiskeys are enough."

Spinelli's band of misfits were quite successful for a while, focusing on small crimes that they figured the police were less likely to investigate. The gang robbed gas stations, picked pockets, stole cars, and sometimes used Gypsy to lure drunken men into a quiet place where the rest of the gang could beat and rob them. Spinelli was the brains behind the operation; she orchestrated the crimes, schooled her young crooks in the fine art of thievery, and even made some of the gang's weapons, such as the blackjacks she skillfully crafted by sewing lead shot into leather pouches. She had also learned nursing skills at some point, and instructed her fellow gang members on the most vulnerable places to smack a victim with one of those handmade blackjacks.

The gang's fortunes turned one fateful day in April of 1940 when the group decided to rob a barbecue stand run by a man named Leland Cash. (It seems like a strange choice for a crime, and one has to wonder if some verbal mix-up led to that decision. Maybe the gang overheard someone say *If you're looking for Cash, you should go to the barbecue stand* and mistakenly thought the place was overflowing with money.) During the robbery, the half-blind Albert Ives demanded that the half-deaf Leland Cash hand over all of his—well, cash. When the barbecue stand owner reached into his pocket to turn up the volume on his hearing aid, Ives panicked and shot the man, killing him.

The gang had beaten up plenty of victims, but had never taken a life before. The person most affected by it turned out to be the teenager Robert Sherrod; he babbled on and on about the murder whenever the gang was together, and even mentioned the crime to his brother's fiancée. Spinelli and her cronies decided that Sherrod had to be bumped off before he got them all arrested, but no one could agree on the method. They discussed shooting him, beating him to death, driving over him with a car, and even tying him to some nearby railroad tracks before the Duchess came up with a kinder, gentler plan of action. One day while the gang was drinking whisky in their hideout, Spinelli sneaked some knockout drops into Sherrod's glass. Once the drugs started to take effect, the Duchess and her cronies beat Sherrod into unconsciousness. Then the gang wrestled him into a pair of swim trunks and dumped him in a nearby river, figuring the cops would think Sherrod had drowned.

Sherrod's body was actually discovered faster than the gang had hoped, but the fact that he had no water in his lungs ruled out drowning as a possible cause of death. The police began an investigation, which made the gang nervous and wary of each other. During a road trip to Reno, Albert Ives got the feeling that he might be the next person the Duchess bumped off since he was the shooter in the barbecue stand robbery and therefore the one the law was most anxious to get their hands on. After overhearing a conversation where Spinelli mentioned the possibility of pushing Ives off a 700-foot cliff, the one-eyed crook ran away from his comrades, turned himself in to the police, and told them everything about the Cash and Sherrod murders.

Before long, the entire gang was behind bars. Ives turned state's evidence and vomited out information about every crime the gang had ever committed, which didn't leave the Duchess or the others with much wiggle room after they were arrested. The trunk of the gang's car had been loaded with weapons when the cops pulled them over, and Spinelli was still carrying the gun Ives had used to kill Leland Cash in her purse. The Duchess first feigned innocence and then tried to blame the crimes on the other gang members—including her daughter Gypsy, who was pregnant by then—but neither the police nor the courts were fooled. Spinelli, Simeone, and Hawkins were all found guilty of first degree murder for Sherrod's death and were sentenced to die in the gas chamber.

Despite the Duchess's long criminal background, the thought of executing a woman gave law enforcement officials the jitters. Spinelli received three reprieves while she waited for her execution day to arrive, but the governor finally realized he couldn't stretch the nasty business out any longer. The Duchess remained mostly stoic throughout the ordeal, but when she found out she had run out of reprieves, she told the governor and her jailers that she hoped her blood would burn holes in all those who had condemned her. Spinelli was the first member of the gang to die, entering the gas chamber with photos of her children and her grandchild pinned to her shirt. Simeone and Hawkins were executed one week later in a double-header. Ironically, Albert "One-Eye" Ives was found not guilty by reason of insanity and spent the rest of his years resting in an asylum, making him the sole member of the Duchess's gang to receive the "royal treatment," even though he was the only one directly involved in both murders.

Karla Faye Tucker

Karla Faye Tucker was a woman with an axe to grind—literally. And while she sure could pick her friends, she could also pick her enemies. That disturbing trait would eventually land her on death row, where she became a media darling and cellblock celebrity before her controversial and highly-publicized execution put an end to all those guest appearances on TV.

Tucker grew up in a fractured household; her parents frequently divorced and remarried each other, mainly because of extramarital affairs. One of those dalliances created Karla Faye, and even though her mother, her two sisters, and her "father" treated her like a true member of the family, the illegitimate Tucker would always feel a little like an outsider. She was exceptionally close to her mother, a habitual drug abuser, and those bad habits rubbed off on a young Karla Faye when she was only eight years old.

At an age when most girls were rolling their dolls around in strollers, Tucker was rolling her own joints. She was also popping pills and smoking cigarettes, and by the time she turned 10 she had already shot heroine for the first time. By the age of 12, Tucker was having sex with a member of the Banditos, a local biker gang. At 14 she had dropped out of school, was turning tricks, and enjoyed tagging along with her rock groupie mother as she followed bands like the Eagles and the Allman Brothers from city to city.

By 1983, Tucker was a tough, scrappy little firecracker who loved to party and was up to her elbows in the biker lifestyle. On the night of the murders that would lead Tucker to the death chamber, she was in the midst of a three-day drugfest/orgy thrown to celebrate the birthday of one of her sisters. After consuming mass quantities of methadone, Valium, Quaaludes, cocaine, bathtub speed, beer, whisky, rum, tequila, marijuana, heroin, and half a dozen pain killers and sedatives, Tucker became morose as she talked with her best friend Shawn Dean, who had recently divorced her husband Jerry Lynn Dean. Tucker had been mad at Jerry since the night he parked his motorcycle in her living room and leaked oil onto the carpet, and now she was steamed at him for giving Shawn a farewell beating before the couple split up.

In the wee hours of the morning, Tucker and her boyfriend Daniel Garrett came up with a plan to break into Jerry Dean's home and steal his prized Harley Davidson. Messing with the man's bike would be the ultimate insult, and a fine way to repay Dean for mistreating his ex-wife. After recruiting another partygoer named James Leibrant, who also hated Dean, the boozy trio dressed in black and headed for Dean's run-down apartment. Because of the late hour, they were hoping Dean would be passed out or asleep by then. The would-be thieves planned to sneak inside, case the joint, then steal the bike if conditions were right. If not, they would at least get a good look at the place and could come back later to snatch the Harley.

While Leibrant stayed outside as a lookout, Tucker and Garrett made their way into the dark apartment. Inside they found Dean's motorcycle, which was partially disassembled and spread out on a tarp along with an assortment of tools. In fact, so many tools were scattered around the place that it looked more like a garage than a home. Even a shovel and pickax were leaning against the wall. Tucker and Garrett were contemplating which pieces of the

Harley to steal first when a light came on in the bedroom and Jerry Dean's voice rumbled out into the living room, asking who the hell was in his apartment. Tucker froze, but Garrett grabbed a hammer from the floor and raced into the bedroom, where he began beating Dean in the head. Tucker watched from the doorway, fascinated, as Garrett bludgeoned Dean again and again. Then, with a wild desire to take part in the bloodlust herself, she snatched the pickax from the living room and rushed into the bedroom.

Dean lay sprawled on the bed, bleeding and unconscious. Beside him, a terrified young woman lay cowering under the covers. Tucker struck Dean with the pickax dozens of times because the injured man's gurgling noises were bothering her, then she turned her focus on the woman, Deborah Thornton. Tucker struck her multiple times as well, and left the pickax buried in the woman's heart. Later, Tucker would claim that she enjoyed the killings so much that she experienced an orgasm with every swing of the bloody weapon.

After the murder victims were discovered, it didn't take long before the police set their sights on Tucker and Garrett. They were both known associates of Jerry Dean, and the bad blood between Dean and

Tucker was legendary. Once investigators began questioning the guests from the drunken orgy, copious amounts of beans were spilled. Garrett's brother, Tucker's sister, Dean's ex-wife, and even James Leibrant himself gave gory details of the gory crime, which Tucker and Garrett had bragged about at the next drunken party. Leibrant eventually turned state's evidence and was granted full immunity for his small part in the crime, while Garrett and Tucker were both found guilty of murder and sentenced to death.

Garrett died in prison of liver disease before he could be executed, but Tucker wasn't so fortunate. During the 14 years she spent on death row, however, Tucker did everything she could to have her sentence commuted to life in prison. After stealing a bible from a jailhouse puppet show (because she didn't know prisoners could request free bibles), Tucker claimed to see the light. She became an active Christian who attracted the attention of luminaries such as Pope John Paul II and televangelist Pat Robertson, and she even married a man named Dana Lane Brown, who worked as both a prison minister and a car dealer. Tucker was a cute, bubbly woman who alternated between spouting bible verses and spouting remorse for her crimes. She became the poster child for the anti-execution movement and the guest that every talk show host in America yearned to interview. The media spotlight aimed at Tucker was even brighter than the heavenly faith she had claimed to find in prison.

But Tucker didn't spend all her jail time doing interviews and lobbying for an appeal; while she was incarcerated, Tucker took part in one of the most bizarre state-sponsored fund raising campaigns ever. The pickax murderess was convicted at the height of the Cabbage Patch Kids craze, when both children and adults across the USA clamored to buy the little squishy-faced dolls that came with unique names and adoption papers. Someone thought it would be a great idea for the women on Texas's death row to make similar dolls, which they called Parole Pals. These looked nearly identical to Cabbage Patch Kids, but instead of coming with adoption papers, each doll came with a parole certificate. They weren't for sale to the public, but employees of the state government could order dolls of a specific gender with whatever hair color, eye color, and clothing they desired. Tucker and the other female death row inmates spent six hours a day knitting and sewing to keep up with the high demand for the popular dolls.

I'm not sure which aspect of this bothers me more;

the fact that death row inmates had daily access to sewing needles, knitting needles, and other items that could easily be used as a deadly weapon, or the wild popularity of dolls with a criminal background. I think it's safe to say that both are pretty disturbing.

While Tucker went about her business of sewing delinquent dolls, exercising, reading, and doing whatever else she could to kill time, her lawyers filed numerous appeals and requests for retrials. Rumors swirled that the woman would have her sentence commuted, either by the Supreme Court or by then-governor George W. Bush. After all, Texas hadn't executed a woman since the Civil War days. But clemency wasn't in the cards for Tucker, and in the end the born-again butcher did indeed die at the hands of the state. On February 3, 1998, Tucker received a lethal injection of sodium thiopental, pancuronium bromide, and potassium chloride—which sounds far less dangerous than a mixture of methadone, Valium, Quaaludes, cocaine, bathtub speed, beer, whisky, rum, tequila, marijuana, heroin, and half a dozen pain killers and sedatives—but the results would prove otherwise.

Martha Beck

In the prison world, a death sentence is the heaviest weight an inmate ever has to bear. But if an inmate is already dealing with "weighty issues," the looming specter of capital punishment can seem like even more of a hefty burden. Such was the case with Martha Beck, a lonely, lovesick, and calorically-challenged nurse who traded in her romance novels and bonbons for a life of crime then paid the ultimate price for it.

Beck was born in Milton, Florida, in 1920. She was a heavy child with a glandular condition that caused her to mature unnaturally fast, so by the age of 10 Beck had already entered puberty. Combined with her excess weight, this caused Beck to be ridiculed by both her classmates and her own family members. Despite her personal problems, however, Beck performed well in high school then went on to nursing school, where she graduated at the top of her class. Those good grades didn't guarantee a job in her chosen field, though, as many employers turned Beck down based on her appearance alone. Beck did work for a short period as an undertaker's assistant, where she was tasked with preparing female bodies for burial (and it's worth noting that not a single client complained about her performance during that time).

Bored to death by her grave work situation, Beck moved to California and found a job at an Army hospital. She also spent her evenings trolling the bars for companionship, displaying a sexual appetite just as robust as her regular appetite. Beck wound up pregnant after a drunken one-night stand and hoped the circumstances would lead to marriage, but the father-to-be threw himself into the ocean instead of proposing. The suicide attempt failed, but the man still wanted nothing to do with Beck so she returned home to Florida, pregnant and heartbroken. Embarrassed by her circumstances, she lied to her friends and family by inventing a story about a husband in the Navy who had been killed in action. Beck gave birth to a daughter, and soon afterward she was pregnant again following a dalliance with a bus driver. This time the father did reluctantly propose, but the loveless marriage only lasted six months before Beck found herself divorced and with two small children.

Still desperate to find love—and a husband who would stay with her for more than a few months—Beck placed an ad in *Mother Dinene's Family Club for Lonely Hearts*, a publication for single men and women seeking companionship. Beck continued to devour both romance novels and chocolate while she waited for a reply, but her mailbox remained empty. Then, after what seemed like an eternity, Beck received a letter from Raymond Fernandez, a successful businessman from New York who was also eager for marriage. Beck was ecstatic that an eligible man was finally interested in her. What she didn't realize, however, was that Fernandez was a con man who had been seducing lonely women then robbing them of their cash and valuables for months.

After exchanging a few letters, Fernandez traveled to Florida to meet Martha in person. The two spent several passionate days together before Fernandez returned to New York with all the information about Beck's financial assets tucked secretly away. When Fernandez sent Beck another letter saying he had changed his mind about having a relationship with her, Beck's grief was so strong she nearly killed herself. When Fernandez found out, he broke with his normal routine and invited Beck to visit him in New York. That two-week vacation seemed like heaven to Beck, and when she returned to Florida and found out that she had been fired from her job, Beck turned right around and went back to New York with her two kids in tow.

Fernandez was flummoxed when Beck and her children showed up at his door. Con men didn't have steady girlfriends—especially ones with kids—but Fernandez enjoyed the way Beck cooked for him, cleaned for him, and took care of his every need. He liked Beck's companionship so much, in fact, that he made her an offer: if she ditched the kids, she could stay with him. Beck responded by dropping the kids off at the local Salvation Army like a couple of worn-out sweaters, then happily returned to her man. Impressed by this show of loyalty, Fernandez confessed everything to Beck. He described his con scheme, gave details about all the women he had robbed, and even revealed that he had a real wife in Spain who knew nothing about his illegal activities. Fernandez expected Beck to be disgusted, but instead she seemed impressed and even offered to become her lover's partner-in-crime.

A stunned but happy Fernandez took Beck up on her offer. Together, the two continued Fernandez's con game with Beck helping to pick the victims and sometimes posing as Fernandez's sister to give him extra credibility. They stole money, cars, and other valuables, leaving behind a trail of lonely female victims who were too embarrassed to go to the police after they were robbed by their new paramour. Beck was a willing, enthusiastic participant in the crimes, although she always did her best to make sure Fernandez didn't consummate any of the new relationships he formed. But Beck's jealousy got the best of her during one con game when she supposedly entered Fernandez's bedroom and found him naked in bed with Janet Fay, the woman they were currently trying to cheat and rob. Beck claimed that she blacked out for a few minutes, and when she came to her senses again she was holding a ball-peen hammer and the other woman was lying on the floor and bleeding from several head wounds. Beck and Fernandez finished the job by strangling the woman with a scarf, then they stored the body in a large trunk for a few days before they buried it in the basement of a rented house.

Murder had never been part of the con game before, but Beck and Fernandez went about their business as if nothing had changed. The pair left New York and drove to Michigan to meet up with their next victim, a young widow named Delphine Downing who had a two-year-old daughter named Rainelle. Fernandez wooed Delphine in his usual manner, and soon the two were sleeping together—much to the chagrin of Beck, who was once again masquerading as her boyfriend's sister. The con game was going smoothly until the day Delphine freaked out after seeing the normally dashing Fernandez without his toupee on. She accused him of deceiving her, and had to be calmed down with sleeping pills. Rainelle became upset during the incident, and an impatient Beck responded by choking the girl into unconsciousness. Worried that Delphine would notice the girl's bruised neck and call the police after she woke up, Fernandez shot the sleeping woman in the head, killing her. Later, Beck drowned Rainelle in a tub of water after the pair couldn't figure out how to stop the girl from crying. They buried both bodies in the basement, then went to see a movie. Later that evening, as the couple were preparing to move on to another town, police showed up at the house. They had been called by one of the neighbors, who had noticed the suspicious goings-on.

The con game was over, and the killers were caught. But after being duped into believing they would be tried and convicted in Michigan, which didn't have the death penalty, Fernandez and Beck confessed freely to their laundry list of crimes, including all the sordid details. The killers were also promised they might serve only a few years in prison if they told the truth and cooperated with police, which seemed like a deal too good to be true. Once the newspapers began running stories about the plus-sized murderess and her suave boyfriend, however, things started to get ugly. The pair were dubbed the Honeymoon Killers, the Lonely Hearts Killers, and the Serial Killer Couple. Reporters were also obsessed with Beck's size, referring to her as Big Martha, Fat Martha, the Fat Lady, and the Triple-Chinned Killer. One paper even described her as "a 200-pound figure of wrath." Bowing to public pressure, Michigan authorities finally allowed New York to extradite the couple and try them for the murder of their first victim, Janet Fay, which meant they would face the death penalty after all.

During the trial—which resembled a three-ring circus more than a court proceeding—Fernandez and Beck alternated between defending each other and accusing each other. They also tried to retract the statements they gave in Michigan, complaining that they had been swindled by the cops with promises of light jail sentences in return for full confessions. But the damning evidence had already been collected, and the graphic descriptions of sex and violence during their testimonies were so vivid that some ladies had to leave the courtroom. By the time the dust had settled and any spectators who passed out had been revived, Fernandez and Beck had both been found guilty of first degree murder and both were sentenced to die in the electric chair.

On the eve of the execution, New York electrocuted four inmates in a row. The "opening act" consisted of two petty crooks who had killed an airline clerk. Next came Fernandez, who had boasted earlier that day that he would die like a man, but who was so frightened that he had to be forcibly carried to the electric chair. A short time afterward, Beck was escorted to the death chamber. It took some effort, but she finally managed to squeeze her massive frame into Ol' Sparky. She could only manage to mutter *So long* before the switch was thrown, but earlier that day the condemned woman had released a more lengthy final statement:

What does it matter who is to blame? My story is a love story, but only those tortured with love can understand what I mean. I was pictured as a fat, unfeeling woman…I am not unfeeling, stupid, or moronic…in the history of the world, how many crimes have been attributed to love?

Heavy words indeed, from a woman who never took anything lightly.

Angelina Rodriguez

Angelina Rodriguez had a devil of a time deciding what to do for a living. She managed a fast food restaurant, sold insurance, earned a cosmetology license, and even tried serving in the Air Force and the Army National Guard. Rodriguez finally decided that the best way to earn a stream of steady income was through fraud, with a dash of murder on the side. The one thing she didn't count on was getting caught—which is surprising, considering the fact that she might have never been arrested or convicted if she hadn't opened her big mouth.

Rodriguez grew up in a somewhat chaotic household in Queens, New York. Her truck driver father abandoned his wife and kids, and her mother worked long hours as a nurse to provide for the family. That meant several other relatives were tasked with babysitting, including Rodriguez's grandfather. The man abused and molested several girls in the family, including Rodriguez, and by the time she was 8 years old the girl had already attempted suicide. She tried again at age 16 and was hospitalized for depression afterward.

Ready to strike out on her own and get away from her depressing family life, Rodriguez married a boy from her neighborhood at age 19 but divorced him shortly thereafter. She then moved to Florida and married again, and within two years she gave birth to two daughters. The marriage seemed heavenly, but disaster would soon strike when the youngest daughter, only 13 months old, choked to death when her pacifier came apart in her mouth. Rodriguez wasted no time in suing the manufacturer and walked away with $250,000. That case would come back to haunt her in later years, although at the time no one seemed to wonder why the grieving mother had also taken out a $50,000 life insurance policy on her baby a few weeks before the tragic "accident."

Rodriguez and her husband divorced shortly afterward, but it didn't take long before Rodriguez was married again—and divorced again, only months later. But in 2000 she would meet the man who became her fourth and final husband, the man whose death would change Rodriguez's life forever.

Rodriguez met Frank Rodriguez—whose name she would later take—when both were working at the Angel Gate Academy near Los Angeles. The place was a boot camp for troubled youth, and both Angelina and Frank were employed as platoon sergeants there. The romance was another whirlwind one for Angelina, and two months after they met the pair were already married. Barely three months after the ceremony, Angelina convinced Frank to buy a $250,000 life insurance policy that named her as the sole beneficiary. When talking to a friend about her husband's new policy, Angelina remarked, "I ought to just kill him and get it over with." The friend thought Angelina was joking and decided to play along. She brought up a news story about a woman who had poisoned her husband with leaves from an oleander plant, then mentioned a relative who was thinking of using hot dogs soaked in antifreeze to kill a mean neighborhood dog. Angelina seemed quite interested in the topic, and asked plenty of questions.

The month after Frank took out his life insurance policy, Angelina began an affair with an ex-con. Shortly afterward, Frank came home one day to find the house empty and a strange smell in the garage. A service technician came to investigate and discovered two gas leaks, one coming from the water heater and one coming from the clothes dryer. The connections were very loose, as if the hoses had purposefully been unscrewed to cause the leaks. The next month, Frank woke up from a nap complaining of a headache and stomach problems. Authorities believe that Angelina tried to poison him with tea made from oleander, but the concoction only made Frank sick instead. Angelina took Frank to the doctor, who assumed Frank had food poisoning and ordered him to rest and drink plenty of fluids. Angelina followed these instructions to the letter, urging Frank to stay in bed while she brought him soup and Gatorade every few hours. According to prosecutors, however, Angelina was mixing a healthy dose of antifreeze into every glass of the sports drink.

Within two days, Frank was dead. Angelina loudly proclaimed that Frank had been poisoned, and she blamed the crime on one of Frank's coworkers at Angel Gate. She also wasted no time in contacting her insurance company to find out when she could receive the payout on her dead husband's $250,000 policy, but was told that no money could be issued until a cause of death had been determined. Based on Angelina's claims, Frank's blood was tested for both common poisons and drugs that can cause an overdose, but no traces of either were found.

Irritated, Angelina tried her best to steer investigators in the right direction by mentioning oleander. When that didn't work, she made up an elaborate lie about receiving an anonymous phone call from someone at Angel Gate who knew details about Frank's murder. This nameless voice supposedly urged Angelina to tell the police to look for antifreeze in Frank's blood. They did, and found a full 12 ounces in the dead man's body—roughly six times the amount that would kill a grown man.

It would have been impossible not to suspect Angelina of the crime. Not only did she seem calm and unemotional when she spoke about her husband's death, but she had clearly lied about the anonymous phone call about the antifreeze (no such call showed up in her phone records) and there was also no evidence that a coworker at Angel Gate might have committed the crime. To make matters worse, Angelina had a long history of collecting both insurance payments and court-ordered settlements; in addition to the settlement from the pacifier case, she had also sued a fast food restaurant for sexual harassment and a department store for negligence after she supposedly fell and hurt herself in a dressing room. The woman's eager pursuit of her freshly-dead husband's insurance money was just the poisoned icing on the deadly cake.

Angelina was arrested on charges of first-degree murder, and as she sat in a cell awaiting trial, the evidence continued to mount up against her. First Angelina tried unsuccessfully to arrange the killing of the friend she had first discussed oleander and antifreeze poisoning with. Then investigators revisited the case of Angelina's daughter who choked to death and concluded that Angelina had torn off part of the pacifier and shoved it down her baby's throat. But Angelina denied all these claims, and in court she even suggested that her husband had committed suicide by drinking antifreeze on purpose.

"How could I have gotten all that green goop into this intelligent man?" she asked the judge. "I might have been depressed. I might have been sad. But I'm not an idiot."

Prosecutors disagreed, however, with one deputy district attorney remarking, "Her relentlessness in her effort to pursue her goals was matched only by her stupidity."

Other law enforcement officials concurred. If Angelina hadn't brought up the possibility of poisoning and then named the exact toxins used in the crime, she might have never been a suspect. "Her talking to us? That was the difference," claimed one homicide detective. "We might never have solved the case if she wasn't talking."

Although she never confessed to her crime, merely rolling her eyes and tapping her foot as her sentence was read, Angelina was found guilty of first degree murder and received the death penalty. How ironic that the woman who spent her whole life trying to force others to pay up must now pay the ultimate price herself.

Christa Pike

Most death row denizens perform their outrageous antics before they're incarcerated; afterward, when confined to a tiny cell with minimal opportunities for mischief, they tend to enter a sedentary state where staring at the walls and seething at society are the top two activities in their day planners. But for Christa Pike, convicted of a crime just as brazen as it was brutal, the stream of hijinks continues as the sands of time trickle with agonizing slowness toward her eventual execution date.

Pike grew up in a dysfunctional household in West Virginia, raised by an abusive and alcoholic grandmother. After her grandmother died, Pike shuffled back and forth between her mother's home and father's home, but never bonded with either. According to family members, Pike started growing her own marijuana at age 9 and had a live-in boyfriend at age 14. She would soon drop out of high school, and although she managed to steer clear of the law, her father described her as violent, dishonest, and manipulative.

At age 18, Pike enrolled in computer programming classes at the Job Corps Center in Knoxville, Tennessee. While there, Pike became romantically involved with another student named Tadaryl Shipp, a dashing young man who also dabbled in the occult (Shipp's nickname was Baby Satan, and his pet name for Pike was Lil Devil). One day, Pike remarked to another student that she wanted to kill someone that day because she "just felt mean." For her victim, Pike picked a student named Colleen Slemmer. Bad blood had been simmering between the two for a while—probably because Pike thought Slemmer wanted to steal Shipp away from her—so Pike came up with a plan to get rid of her "rival" once and for all.

Accompanied by another female student, Shadolla Peterson, Pike and Shipp lured Slemmer into a secluded spot in the woods by offering her marijuana. Once the group was alone in the forest, Pike began hitting and kicking Slemmer. Soon Shipp joined in, which is when the pair switched to deadlier weapons. Pike used a box cutter to slash Slemmer dozens of times, then she pulled out a miniature meat cleaver she had borrowed from an acquaintance. Slemmer was cut and slashed again and again, until Pike finally grabbed a chunk of asphalt from the ground and used it to bludgeon Slemmer to death.

When the body was found two days later, there were so many wounds that the medical examiner had a hard time listing them all. In addition to countless cuts and stab wounds, the victim had pentagrams carved on her chest and forehead. Her face had been so badly beaten that she was unrecognizable.

Connecting Pike to the crime was probably the simplest task local law enforcement had ever encountered. The girl had bragged about the killing to a fellow student, recounting the brutal details in a sing-song voice as she danced happily around the room. Pike also told her friend that she had taken part of Slemmer's skull as a souvenir, then pulled a piece of bone wrapped in a napkin out of her jacket pocket and proudly displayed it. Pike later told the story to a second student, who was also shown the skull fragment. "And that ain't mud on my shoes, that's blood," Pike boasted. Later, Pike revisited the crime scene and giggled as she asked police officers for details about the case. One of the men noticed that Pike was wearing a pentagram necklace, identical to the symbol carved into the victim's flesh.

Pike's room and Shipp's room were eventually searched, and police found an altar, a Satanic bible, and other damning evidence. They also found the piece of Slemmer's skull in the pocket of Pike's jacket, which she had left in a school counselor's office by mistake.

Pike didn't even attempt to deny her role in the killing, but she did tell police that she and the others were only trying to scare Slemmer before the situation got out of control. She then gave a 46-page confession that contained every gory detail of the hideous crime. At her trial, Pike cried when these details were revisited. Those courtroom tears and her baby face didn't sway the jury, however, and Pike was found guilty of murder and sentenced to death. Shipp, who was only 17 when the crime was committed, was also found guilty and received a life sentence because of his age. Because Peterson had informed on Pike and Shipp, she was given probation for her small role as an accessory to the crime.

Once the trial was over, Pike's mask of innocence and regret slipped off. In a letter she wrote to Shipp shortly after her conviction, Pike complained, *Ya see what I get for trying to be nice to the hoe? I went ahead and bashed her brains out so she'd die quickly instead of letting her bleed to death and suffer more, and they fuckin FRY me!!! Ain't that some shit.*

At the time, Pike was the youngest woman on death row in America. Reporters clamored for interviews with the baby-faced killer, and when the cameras were rolling, Pike spoke in a soft southern accent as thick and sweet as molasses. She showed off her death row cell, decorated with butterflies, angels, and stuffed animals. She talked about her fear of the electric chair. She lamented the fact that she wasn't out in the real world, going to school or working or hanging out with her friends. And while she never gushed with remorse, she tried nonetheless to portray herself as a sympathetic character.

That act didn't last long at all. Pike became quite the prolific letter writer while in prison, and one of her new pen pals was fellow convicted killer John Lee Fryman, incarcerated in Ohio. Pike sent long, descriptive letters to Fryman filled with details of her love for violence and death. *I like to see blood and brains*, Pike wrote. *Fatty tissues and wide open ripped flesh.* Another letter confessed, *I have this great need to be physical with another human being. Be it good or evil I care not. Sex or murder. To hold a child or slit a grown man's abdomen open and watch his guts fall to the ground. What's wrong with me?* Pike also mailed graphic love letters to other men, making promises such as *I want to lick your soul* and sometimes including a lock of hair or a pair of worn panties, which wound up for sale on the internet. One of her pen pals became so enamored that he plotted to break Pike out of jail, bribing a guard with a canoe and a guitar in exchange for copies of prison keys. Other guards discovered the plot while it was still in the planning stages, however, and the scheme was quickly thwarted.

While in prison, Pike's love for violence wasn't merely confined to her letters. Less than five years after she was sentenced to death, Pike was tried and convicted for attempted murder after she tried to strangle a fellow prisoner with a shoelace. Even though Pike was already slated to die, a judge added an additional 25 years to her jail sentence as a warning to other inmates that such behavior wouldn't be tolerated.

Even after the second attempted murder, and despite the fact that Pike's letters glorifying violence were all turned over to law enforcement officials, Pike's lawyers continue to appeal her death sentence to this day. The most recent attempt, in 2015, claimed that executing Pike could be classified as cruel and unusual punishment because she was "a mentally ill, cognitively impaired, immature adolescent" when the murder took place—a murder that included an hour of torture before Pike finally dispatched her victim with a chunk of asphalt. The judge refused to overturn Pike's death sentence, and probably questioned whether the attorney's reality check had gotten lost in the mail.

Christa Pike has yet to receive an execution date, but one thing is for certain; while she'll never spend time with her boyfriend "Baby Satan" again, an impending appointment with the real deal still looms in her future.

Elizabeth Ann Duncan

Contrary to popular belief, mother *doesn't* always know best; especially when that mother is Elizabeth "Ma" Duncan, who orchestrated the cruel murder of her pregnant daughter-in-law because she refused to share her son's affections with another woman—both in and out of the bedroom, according to some rumors.

Little is known of Duncan's early years. She was born sometime around 1904, but few records remain of her school years or her job history. What is known, however, is that Duncan married and divorced somewhere between 10 and 20 times during her life, with some marriages overlapping others whenever Duncan neglected to get a divorce. Some or all of these unions might have been shams, with Duncan luring young men into marriage so she could help herself to their finances. Duncan did have at least two children—and possibly more—as the result of these marriages, but one of the two, a daughter, died from a cerebral hemorrhage at age 15. The remaining child, a son named Frank, became the sole object of Duncan's affection, in ways that many friends and acquaintances found disturbing. Some called it an "unnatural love" or an "unhealthy love" while others were bold enough to label it incest. But whether the relationship was physical or purely emotional, one thing was for certain: Ma Duncan would kill any woman who tried to come between her and her son.

Elizabeth and Frank Duncan lived together in San Francisco until Frank was 28 years old, and despite all the time they spent together at home, Elizabeth followed her son to work as well. Frank was just starting out as a lawyer (Elizabeth supposedly worked as the madam of a brothel to pay for her son's law school), and Ma Duncan would sit in the courtroom while Frank performed his duties, clapping and cheering whenever her son won a case. One day, however, Frank's lawyer buddies intimated that it might be time for Frank to cut the apron strings and settle down with a woman he wasn't already related to. It seemed like a logical idea, but when Frank broached the subject with Ma Duncan, all hell broke loose. The two yelled, screamed, and fought until the battle finally ended with Elizabeth swallowing a fistful of sleeping pills rather than leave the home she shared with Frank. A mad dash to the hospital and a lively session of stomach pumping brought Elizabeth back to the land of the living, however, and that's when things *really* got interesting.

While recovering from her near-overdose, Ma Duncan was assigned a pretty young nurse named Olga Kupczyk. Frank was instantly smitten with Olga, and the two soon began dating. Elizabeth was livid; after she left the hospital, she started calling Olga every day and telling her to leave her son alone. She tried the same tactic with Frank, but her demands that he end the relationship fell on deaf ears. That's when Elizabeth upped the ante, threatening to kill Olga rather than allow her to marry her son. To avoid a bloodbath at the wedding, Frank and Olga decided to marry in secret—but it didn't take long before Ma Duncan found out about the nuptials and showed up on the newlyweds's doorstep, demanding that Frank come home and stay with her. For the next few weeks Frank traveled back and forth between his new apartment and his mother's home, trying to placate both women by splitting his time between them. Olga eventually got fed up with the bizarre situation, though, and demanded that Frank come back to her permanently. Shortly afterward, the new bride announced that she was pregnant.

With a baby on the way, Ma Duncan knew she had to end the marriage—and possibly Olga's life—as quickly as possible. First she hired an ex-con named Ralph Winterstein to accompany her to the local courthouse, where the pair pretended to be Olga and Frank and filed for an uncontested annulment of their marriage. The request was granted, and afterward Ma Duncan asked Winterstein if he might be interested in bumping Olga off. The ex-con refused, so Elizabeth started asking some of Frank's seedy clients if any of them would like to earn some fast cash in exchange for a little murder. Ma Duncan eventually found two men who agreed to do the deed: Luis Moya (a petty crook with offenses dating back to age 11) and Gus Baldonado (a former Army medic who had transitioned from saving lives to taking them). The group came up with a plan for Moya and Baldonado to kidnap Olga, drive her across the border to Tijuana, kill her there, then leave the body in Mexico. Duncan pawned some jewelry then gave the pair of thugs $175 for weapons and travel expenses.

The hired killers rented a car, borrowed a gun, then

showed up at Olga's apartment in Santa Barbara late one night when they knew Frank wouldn't be home. Moya knocked on the door and told Olga he was a friend of Frank's; he claimed that Frank was in the back seat of his car, drunk, and asked Olga to help him get the man inside. Dressed in her pajamas and a bathrobe, the pregnant woman followed Moya to the car and opened the door to the back seat, where Baldonado was hunched over with his face hidden. Moya smacked Olga on the head with his gun, then his partner wrestled the stunned girl into the car.

With their victim on board, the two thugs began the long drive to Tijuana. Olga didn't make it easy for them, though, and because she kept yelling and struggling, her captors had to make frequent pit stops so they could hit her with the borrowed pistol in the hopes of quieting her down. The rental car also gave the pair trouble, so they decided to take an impromptu detour into the mountains rather than risk breaking down on the way to Mexico. Once they reached a quiet, deserted spot, the hired killers planned to shoot Olga then bury her body. Two things hampered their plan, however: first, the pair had beaten Olga with the gun so many times that it was broken and couldn't be fired. Second, neither of the geniuses had thought to toss a shovel in the trunk so they had no tools to dig a grave. Improvising once again, the two thugs took turns strangling Olga then used their hands to scoop out a shallow hole in the ground. Baldonado, the former Army medic, checked Olga's vital signs and announced that she was dead before he pushed her into the grave and the pair drove away.

Olga's coworkers at the hospital reported her missing, and the police began an investigation. While interviewing potential witnesses, Olga's father and her landlady told police about Ma Duncan's constant harassment and death threats. One of Frank's fellow attorneys also stumbled upon the phony marriage annulment around the same time, and Elizabeth was quickly arrested and charged with fraud and forgery. Moya and Baldonado were arrested soon afterward, and the pair sang like proverbial birds. They gave police full details of Olga's murder, and also led them to the body. When medical examiners found dirt in Olga's lungs, they determined that the pregnant girl had still been alive when the inept killers buried her.

Moya, Baldonado, and Ma Duncan were all charged with first degree murder, with Duncan being the only one of the three to maintain her innocence. But considering the fact that she'd threatened Olga's life in front of countless acquaintances—sometimes going into painstaking detail about how she might kill the girl—the jury wasn't convinced. The brutal nature of the murder, combined with the fact that Olga was pregnant at the time, also ensured that Moya, Baldonado, and Ma Duncan all received the death penalty. Three years after the trial ended, the trio were executed in California's gas chamber. Moya and Baldonado went first, with Elizabeth headlining the show. Ironically, Frank wasn't even there to witness the execution because he was in court at the time, tirelessly arguing for a last-minute reprieve for his deadly mother. Even with the Grim Reaper tugging his mom in the opposite direction, Frank just couldn't let go of those apron strings.

Miss Runners-Up: The Women Who Didn't Quite Make It

Just as every beauty pageant has its winner, each of these glamorous events also has a Miss Runner-Up. These are the women who were *nearly* the loveliest, the most poised, the most talented, the most charming. They smile and clap dutifully as Miss Universe or Miss America or Miss World accepts her crown and bouquet of roses, but on the inside they're swearing like sailors and eager to drown their sorrows in a few glasses of wine as they begin a long, sulky evening.

Death row has far less glamour, glitz, and pageantry, but it also has its fair share of Miss Runners-Up. Some of them are women who were awarded the death penalty but then had their sentences overturned or commuted. Others were convicted of brutal crimes but received long jail terms instead of a capital punishment decree. And several were deemed guilty by the public and the press but found innocent by the courts, living out their lives as free women after their murder trials came to an end. But regardless of the way they managed to avoid a date with death, these runners-up shed tears of joy instead of sorrow when the mantle of Miss Death Row was awarded to somebody else.

Lizzie Borden

Every school kid knows the popular playground rhyme that goes like this:

> Lizzie Borden took an axe
>
> And gave her mother forty whacks.
>
> When she saw what she had done
>
> She gave her father forty-one.

And while Lizzie Borden and the crime she was accused of are legendary, many people don't realize that Borden was never convicted of the murders, which remain technically unsolved to this day.

One sweltering summer morning in August of 1892, Andrew Borden and his wife Abby were murdered in their Massachusetts home. Andrew, a wealthy businessman, was found slumped on a couch in his living room. He had been struck on the head 10 to 11 times with a hatchet or an axe, leaving a corpse too grisly to describe. His wife Abby was later discovered in an upstairs bedroom, her skull crushed by 19 blows from a similar weapon. Because the murders looked like an inside job, the number one suspect was 33-year-old daughter Lizzie, who still lived in the house. She had a tense relationship with both her father Andrew and her step-mother Abby, and she had also tried to purchase poison from the local drug store the day before the murders. Lizzie was the only other family member home at the time of the killings (a maid was also in the house), but she claimed to be in the backyard barn looking for fishing equipment when her father was killed.

Based on the confusing and contradictory answers she gave during questioning, Lizzie was arrested and tried for both murders. The problem was, the police had no physical evidence to tie her to the killings. Four hatchets were found in the Borden family basement, but none showed obvious signs of being used in the crimes. Police also didn't find blood on any of Lizzie's clothes, although three days after the murders Lizzie was caught burning one of her dresses because she claimed it was covered with paint stains. During the trial, the defense came up with multiple ways to prove reasonable doubt. They called several witnesses who claimed to see suspicious strangers near the Borden home just prior to the murders. They then questioned Lizzie's older sister Emma, who testified that Lizzie's relationships with her father and stepmother were actually quite cordial, despite any local rumors. They also played up the fact that Lizzie was a genteel woman with a spotless background.

The lack of evidence and Lizzie's upstanding reputation obviously swayed the jury, who took only an hour and a half to find her not guilty—although playground children still sing rhymes about her guilt to this day.

The Manson Family Women

The Tate/LaBianca murders of 1969 gained international attention because of their vicious brutality, yet none of the women involved in the killings were ever put to death. During the span of two evenings, charismatic cult leader Charles Manson sent Susan Atkins, Linda Kasabian, Patricia Krenwinkel, Leslie Van Houten, and two male members of his "family" out to commit violent murders designed to incite social chaos. Seven people were killed during the two-night bloodbath, including actress Sharon Tate, who was eight months pregnant at the time. Some victims were stabbed while others were shot. The murder scenes looked like slaughterhouses, and the Manson followers even used the blood of their victims to write slogans such as *death to pigs* and *helter skelter* on walls and doors.

After Susan Atkins and Charles Manson himself bragged to others about the killings, the family members who took part in the carnage were charged with murder and put on trial. Linda Kasabian, who had acted as driver and lookout but hadn't participated in the murders, turned state's evidence and was granted immunity in exchange for testifying against the others. But the court handed down death sentences to Susan Atkins, Patricia Krenwinkel, and Leslie Van Houten, who didn't help their own causes by giggling when the murders were described in the courtroom or by later threatening the jurors.

Ironically, the death sentences for all three women were overturned the very next year when the death penalty was ruled unconstitutional. Susan Atkins renounced her ties with the Manson Family two years into her sentence and claimed to be a totally reformed born-again Christian, but she was denied parole 18 times during her decades behind bars. Atkins died in prison in 2009, reportedly of brain cancer. Patricia Krenwinkel also tried to distance herself from Manson after she was imprisoned; she now gives dance lessons, teaches other prisoners to read, and even played on the prison volleyball team. She has been up for parole 13 times, but was denied every time just like Atkins. Leslie Van Houten, however, might end up being the sole member of Manson's female gang of killers to ever see sunlight again. In 2016, at her 21st parole hearing, the 66-year-old woman finally received a recommendation of parole from California's parole panel. That decision must be reviewed and approved by the state's governor before Van Houten actually steps foot outside of prison, though, and both lawmakers and the family of Van Houten's victims have voiced strong opposition to it.

Susan Smith

In the fall of 1994, Susan Smith went from being the most sympathetic mother in America to the most hated mother in America in only nine short days. The reason? At the beginning of that time span, the young woman from South Carolina was the victim of a terrible, unspeakable crime—but by the ninth day, she was confirmed as the perpetrator instead.

Smith first attracted media attention as a mother whose two young children had been abducted during a carjacking. According to Smith, an armed black man jumped inside her car while she was stopped at a red light one evening with her three-year-old and fourteen-month-old sons in the back seat. The carjacker forced Smith out of the car then drove away with her children, promising not to hurt them. Police began a massive search for the two boys, but they also started an investigation into Smith's private life as well. They learned that Smith, who was separated from her husband, had a history of depression. She drank too much, she had contemplated or attempted suicide on several occasions, and she was sleeping with several different men at once while she desperately searched for a permanent romantic partner. As reporters from across the country converged on Union, South Carolina, where Smith stood in front of the cameras and tearfully begged the carjacker to return her sons, police began scrutinizing the woman more and more carefully.

After nine days, a sheriff confronted Smith about the inconsistencies in her carjacking story and urged her to tell the truth. Smith did, and her confession was as shocking as it was gut wrenching. The tale about a carjacker was a lie. Smith had been involved with a wealthy man who ended the relationship because he wasn't interested in dating a woman with children. In the hopes of winning her lover back, Smith had let her car roll into a local lake with her two young sons in the back seat. Police searched the lake and found both the car and the two boys, who had died from drowning.

In a heartbeat, Smith became public enemy number one. She was arrested and charged with two counts of murder, and after a speedy five-day trial she was found guilty on both counts. The prosecution asked for the death penalty, but the jury rejected that option and Smith was sentenced to 30 years to life instead.

Being incarcerated apparently hasn't stopped Smith from searching for a boyfriend. Two correctional officers lost their jobs after having sex with Smith behind bars, and the homicidal mother also posted an ad on a personals website used by inmates searching for playmates. "I consider myself to be sensitive, caring, and kind-hearted," Smith wrote in her ad, immediately followed by "I'm currently serving a life sentence on the charge of murder."

Well, at least she's honest about one thing.

Casey Anthony

Casey Anthony's story is similar to Susan Smith's in many regards; in both cases, a mother was accused of killing her own child (or children) after lying about their disappearance first and blaming the crime on someone else. And in both cases, an angry public voiced its demand for justice with screams and cries that echoed across the globe. But the major difference in Anthony's case was the court verdict, a decision that still leaves many scratching their heads.

Casey Anthony was a single mother with a two-year-old daughter who lived with her parents in Orlando, Florida. When Casey—who was 22 at the time—moved out of the house with her daughter Caylee, Casey's parents George and Cindy worried about not being able to spend as much time with their young granddaughter. Weeks stretched by without a visit. Then, over one month after Casey moved away from her parents, she made a shocking confession to them: she claimed that she had left Caylee with a babysitter named Zanny several weeks earlier, and that she herself hadn't seen Caylee in a long time either.

Because Caylee was nowhere to be found and Casey's story sounded fishy to everyone, Casey was arrested and the police began an investigation. Five months later, Caylee's remains were discovered in a wooded area near George and Cindy's house. Casey was charged with first-degree murder, and the most sensational trial of the 21st century kicked off with a noisy bang. The prosecution sought the death penalty and had plenty of ammunition to use against Casey: during the months that Caylee was supposedly missing, Casey had spent her time drinking and partying at nightclubs, getting tattoos, and entering "Hot Body" contests. George and Cindy had both smelled a strong, unpleasant odor in Casey's car shortly after Caylee's disappearance, possibly the result of Casey driving around with a dead body in the trunk. The family's computer had also been used to search for articles on "fool-proof suffocation" and "how to make chloroform."

Casey's defense team fired back with allegations that Casey had been molested by both her father and her brother, and also claimed that Caylee had actually drowned in George and Cindy's swimming pool, with George disposing of the body and covering up the crime. Because medical examiners couldn't determine how Caylee died, the case boiled down to probable cause and a lack of hard evidence. After only ten hours, the jury found Casey Anthony not guilty of all felony charges. The new "most hated mother in America," who had already been tried, convicted, and sentenced to death by millions of TV viewers and social media junkies, had been acquitted by the small group of people whose opinions were the only ones that mattered.

Casey wasn't just awarded Miss Runner-Up at the Death Row Pageant; the jurors decided she never should've been a contestant to begin with.

Jodi Arias

The murder of Travis Alexander is another case that captivated the public and created a three-ring circus atmosphere with a brutal killing at its center stage. It had all the juicy elements that TV and internet audiences love: steamy sex, outrageous courtroom testimony, and a killer who was equally savage and sensuous. That killer was Jodi Arias, a woman who combined good looks with bad behavior to become the most talked-about murderess in recent history.

On June 9, 2008, the body of 30-year-old Travis Alexander was discovered in the shower of his Mesa, Arizona home. Alexander had been shot in the head, stabbed nearly 30 times, and his throat had been slit. Alexander's friends told police about Jodi Arias, an ex-girlfriend of Alexander's who had been stalking and harassing him for months. Police also found recent photos of Arias on Alexander's digital camera and her DNA in a bloody palm print at the crime scene. Arias was arrested, but claimed she hadn't been in Alexander's home on the day of the murder. She later changed her story and said she *had* been in the home that day, but she blamed Alexander's death on two intruders who allegedly broke into the house. Arias would later alter her story a third time, admitting that she did kill Alexander but also claiming that she acted in self-defense.

During her marathon 18 days of testimony, Arias painted a sordid picture of her relationship with Alexander. She said her ex-boyfriend often called her a slut and a whore, and that he enjoyed rough sex and was also a closet pedophile. One of Alexander's fantasies, Arias said, was to dress her up like Little Red Riding Hood, tie her to a tree in the middle of the woods, then have anal sex with her. He also liked her to wear children's Spiderman underwear during their romantic encounters, which Arias claimed was tied to Alexander's attraction to children. On the day of the murder, Arias stated, Alexander's wild behavior went too far. He got mad after Arias dropped his camera, and Arias was forced to fight for her life when Alexander attacked her.

The prosecution disputed those claims with gusto, arguing that Arias had carefully planned the murder in advance. Alexander's gunshot wound, they said, came from a gun stolen from the house where Arias lived with her grandparents just a week earlier. Arias also rented a car before she drove from California to Arizona to visit Alexander just before the murder, possibly to avoid detection and also to keep evidence of the crime out of her own vehicle (when the rental car was returned, its seats were stained with something that looked like Kool-Aid). Combined with the many lies Arias had told and the number of times she had changed her story, prosecutors were convinced that Alexander's murder had been cold and calculated. The jury agreed, and took only 15 hours to find Arias guilty of first-degree murder.

The penalty phase of the trial, however, didn't go as smoothly. Only 8 of the 12 jurors favored giving Arias the death penalty, which resulted in a mistrial when no consensus was reached. More than a year later, a second penalty trial began. That time only one juror shied away from sentencing Arias to death, but that one vote was enough to cause a second mistrial. With the decision now in the judge's hands, Arias was sentenced to life in prison with no possibility of parole.

In many ways, the Jodi Arias trial reveals one of the reasons behind the shortage of women on America's death row. Despite the brutal nature of the murder, and despite the fact that the jury found Arias guilty of the horrific, premeditated crime, there was still hesitation when it came time to mete out punishment. Jodi Arias looked more like a supermodel than a psychopath, and at least a few of the jurors saw her as a woman first and a killer second. Those two mistrials prove that it isn't easy to sentence someone that pretty to death—even when their crimes are revoltingly ugly.

# # #

About the Author

Ty Treadwell has been researching and writing about death penalty cases for over 20 years. His other books on the topic are *Death Row's Oddest Inmates* and *Last Suppers: Famous Final Meals from Death Row*.

Treadwell's mystery and horror stories have appeared in a variety of magazines, and are collected in the book *Down a Crooked Road; Tales of Mystery & Suspense*. Treadwell is also the author of the mystery novels *The Devil Did Grin* and *Secret 77*. All of his books are available from Amazon, iTunes, Barnes & Noble, Smashwords, and other online retailers.

Also by Ty Treadwell

Last Suppers: Famous Final Meals from Death Row by Ty Treadwell & Michelle Vernon

One death row inmate requested 24 tacos, 6 enchiladas, and 6 tostadas. Another wanted wild rabbit, biscuits, and blackberry pie. And a two-time murderer asked for a can of SpaghettiOs then complained to the press when he didn't get it!

Newly revised and updated, this 10th anniversary edition contains dozens of intriguing last meals ranging from succulent steak and lobster to the lump of dirt ordered by a former voodoo priest. But Last Suppers is more than just a list of meals; you'll also be treated to weird execution facts, prison recipes, and other tidbits of trivia from America's toughest cell blocks. Ever wondered how the last meal tradition began, or what the most popular entrees are among condemned diners? Curious about the lives and loves of capital punishment's fairer sex, the Death Row Dames? Are you craving a taste of Texas Jailhouse Chili, but don't have the recipe? Dying to know what Ted Bundy, John Wayne Gacy, and other famous serial killers ate before their demise? Then pull up a chair, tuck in that bib, and enjoy!

Death Row's Oddest Inmates
by Ty Treadwell

Robert Vickers killed his prison cellmate because the other man drank his Kool-Aid. Varnall Weeks believed that after his execution he would be reincarnated as a giant turtle who would rule the universe. Hit man and former Elvis impersonator James Paster tried to escape from his cell by slathering himself with hair tonic and squeezing through a tiny air vent.

Death Row's Oddest Inmates features 13 of the most bizarre and unique killers the prison system has ever seen. Meet a man who wore a homemade toga during his trial and asked for the bodies of his victims to be brought to the courtroom so God could resurrect them. Learn how triple murderer "Smelly Kelly" earned his nickname, and read about the sadistic serial killer who sued the state of California for cruel and unusual punishment because one of the cookies on his prison lunch tray was broken.

Also included are special sections on wacky murder weapons, massive last meals, and the looniest last words ever uttered. Despite the glum surroundings, there's no shortage of silliness on death row.

The Devil Did Grin
by Ty Treadwell

Some people say *When life gives you lemons, make lemonade*. Will Deacon says, *When life gives you lemons, throw those lemons back at life as hard as you can, and if life ends up with bumps on its head and lemon juice in its eye, it really can't complain because it's the one that gave you those stupid lemons in the first place.*

Former private detective Will Deacon is jobless, aimless, and hasn't traveled more than two blocks from his Atlanta condo in nearly a year—but he's never been happier. A survivor of countless failed careers and one and a half failed marriages, Will is perfectly content to stay holed up at home with only a cat named Socrates for company. But that blissful life comes to an end when the son of an old friend commits suicide. The pampered teen had no reason to kill himself, so Will is dragged out of retirement to find the answer. As he delves into the boy's hidden lifestyle, Will finds himself up against a sleek drug dealer, two frightening hit men, and the head of the Dixie Mafia. When the evidence points to murder instead of suicide, Will is caught in a whirlwind of shocking discoveries and dark family secrets as he tries to solve the most important case of his career.

Down a Crooked Road:
Tales of Mystery & Suspense
by Ty Treadwell

Take the last sharp turn on a crooked road and you might find yourself face to face with a desperate killer, or a clever con man, or a restless spirit whose face is eerily familiar. In the tradition of The Twilight Zone, the 12 stories in this collection all share one common trait; each one ends with a delicious, unexpected twist.

In "The Woman Upstairs," a claustrophobic housewife uses extreme measures to escape from both a cramped apartment and a confining marriage. "The Sorrow Business" tells how a devious reporter suffers the consequences after hounding a murder victim's family for an interview. And in "Deep in the Roaring Fork," a man lost in the backwoods of Colorado stumbles across a lonely tavern whose bartender knows far too many details about his life — and about his death. Includes 7 stories previously published in mystery magazines like *Over My Dead Body* and *Unreality*, as well as 5 brand new stories from award-winning writer Ty Treadwell.

Find Ty Treadwell on the web at:

www.tytreadwell.com

www.lastsuppersbook.blogspot.com

www.deathrowsoddestinmates.blogspot.com

Printed in Great Britain
by Amazon